TRIAL OF THE TWELVE SPANISH PIRATES

OF THE

Schooner PANDA, a Guinea Slaver,

CONSISTING OF

DON PEDRO GIBERT, Captain; Bernardo de Soto, Mate; Francisco Ruiz, Carpenter; Antonio Ferrer, the tattooed Cook; Nicola Costa, Manuel Boyga, Domingo de Guzman, Juan Antonio Portana, Manuel Castillo, Angel Garcia, Jose Velazquez, and Juan Montenegro, Seamen,

For Robbery and Piracy, committed on board the Brig Mexican, 20th Sept. 1832.

The Black King, at Cape Lopez, who protected the Crew of the Panda.

BOSTON:
PUBLISHED BY LEMUEL GULLIVER, 82, STATE STREET.

1834.

A Pirate's Long Knife.

UNITED STATES CIRCUIT COURT.

His Honor JOSEPH STORY, LL. D. } Presiding.
" " JOHN DAVIS, LL. D. }

Counsel for the Government, ANDREW DUNLAP, Esq., District Attorney.

Counsel for the Prisoners, DAVID LEE CHILD, Esq. GEORGE S. HILLARD, Esq.

His Excellency Don Antonio G. Vega, *Spanish Consul.*
Stephen Badlam, Esq. *Sworn Interpreter.*
William H. Payton, Esq., Joseph Tavers, Esq., *Interpreters of the Spanish and Portuguese Languages.*
Jonas L. Sibley, Esq. *Marshal.*
Horatio Bass, Esq., *Deputy Marshal.*

Boston, Tuesday, Nov. 11, 1834, at 9 o'clock A. M., the prisoners, consisting of Don Pedro Gibert, and his mate Bernardo De Soto, with ten of his crew chained together in pairs, were placed at the bar.

The Clerk then read the indictment in English, and Mr. Badlam read it to the prisoners in Spanish.

Indictment.

"At a Circuit Court of the United States of America for the first Circuit, begun and holden at Boston, within and for the District of Massachusetts, on the fifteenth day of October, in the year of our Lord one thousand eight hundred and thirty four, the jurors for the said United States, within and for the said District of Massachusetts, upon their oath present that Pedro Gibert, late of Boston, in said District, Master mariner, Bernardo de Soto, Francisco Ruiz, Nicola Costa, Antonio Ferrer, Manuel Boyga, Domingo de Guzman, Juan Antonio Portana, Manuel Castillo, Angel Garcia, Jose Velazquez, late of Boston in said District, mariners, and Juan Montenegro, late of Boston in said District, mariner, otherwise called Jose Basilio de Castro, late of Boston in said District, mariner, on the twentieth day of September, in the year of our Lord one thousand eight hundred and thirty-two, upon the high sea within the admiralty and maritime jurisdiction of the United States, and out of the jurisdiction of any particular State, with force and arms did feloniously and piratically set upon, board, break and enter a certain merchant brig of the United States, called the Mexican, then and there belonging and appertaining to Joseph Peabody, then being a citizen of the United States, and then and there piratically and feloniously did assault John Groves Butman, then and there being in and on board said brig, and then and there being the Master of said brig, and then and there being a citizen of the United States, and then and there being in the peace of God and the said United States, and did then and there in and on board said brig upon the high sea, within the admiralty and maritime jurisdiction of the United States, and out of the jurisdiction of any particular State, put the said John Groves Butman in great bodily fear and danger of his life; and ten boxes, each containing two thousand dollars of the value of two thousand dollars, and all of the value of twenty thousand dollars; of the goods, chattels, monies, and property of the said Joseph Peabody, then and there being in and laden on board the said brig upon the high sea within the Admiralty and maritime jurisdiction of the United States, and out of the jurisdiction of any particular State, and then and there being under the care, custody and in the possession of the said John Groves Butman, with force and arms from the care, custody and possession of the said John Groves Butman, they the said Pedro Gibert, Bernardo de Soto, Francisco Ruiz, Nicola Costa, Antonio Ferrer, Manuel Boyga, Domingo de Guzman, Juan Antonio Portana, Manuel Castillo, Angel Garcia, Jose Velazquez, Juan Montenegro, otherwise called Jose Basilio de Castro, then and there in the said brig upon the high sea within the Admiralty and maritime jurisdiction of the United States, and out of the jurisdiction of any particular State, piratically, feloniously, violently and against the will of the said John Groves Butman, did steal, rob, take and carry away in the presence of the said John Groves Butman, against the peace and diginty of the said United States, and contrary to the form of the Statutes of the said United States in such case made and provided."

To this indictment the prisoners one and all plead *Not Guilty.*

The Clerk then proceeded to empannel the Jury for the trial; and the following Jurors, after *eighteen* were peremptorily challenged by Don Pedro Gibert, and *twenty* by Bernardo De Soto, were sworn.

Jury.

Charles Lawrence, *Foreman.*	Isaac K. Wise.
Jeremiah Washburn.	Thacher R. Raymond.
Charles Hudson.	William Knight.
Leavitt Covett.	Peter Brigham.
Joseph Kelley.	Jacob H. Bates.
Anthony Kelley.	John Beal.

The *District Attorney* now opened the cause on the part of the government in substance as follows:

May it please your Honors and Gentlemen of the Jury,

On this solemn occasion twelve men of a foreign nation, unacquainted with our language, are placed at the bar of this tribunal to answer for the crime of piracy, or robbery, and depredation on the high seas. This is an offence against the universal law of society;—a pirate being, according to Sir Edward Coke, *hostis humani generis.* As therefore he has renounced all the benefits of society and government, and has reduced himself afresh to the savage state of nature, by declaring war against all mankind, all mankind must declare war against him; so that every community hath a right, by the rule of self defence, to inflict that punishment upon him which every individual would in a state of nature have been otherwise entitled to do, for any invasion of his person or personal property. Piracy is every where pursued and punished with death. It is of no importance, for the purpose of giving jurisdiction in cases of piracy, on whom or where a piratical offence is committed. A pirate who is one by the law of nations may be tried and punished in any country where he may be found, for he is reputed to be out

The Panda standing through the Bahama Channel.

of the protection of all laws. Thus if the prisoners were convicted of the crime for which they are now indicted in their own country, the punishment would be the same as in this, and all civilized nations, which is death.

By the Act of Congress, April 30, 1790, if any person, upon the high seas, or in any river, haven, or bay, out of the jurisdiction of any particular state, commit murder or robbery, on board a vessel, he shall be deemed a pirate and a felon, and shall suffer death. Since then two additional acts have been passed, both of which make the punishment of this offence capital.

A piratical vessel may sail under pretence of being engaged in commerce, having lawful papers; or with a commission from some nation for a specific purpose; and when so engaged commit the crime of Piracy. The celebrated Capt. Kidd sailed under a commission to take Pirates in the Indian Seas, and when so engaged he captured and robbed a Mahometan ship, for which offence he was taken and sent to England, tried and hung in chains at Execution Dock.

After defining the statutes and quoting the precedents applicable to the present case to be found in the books, he gave a brief and pertinent detail of the robbery and piracy on board the Mexican: which he expected to prove in the case. Also the capture of the prisoners by an English Brig of War: and their subsequent conveyance to this country. He concluded, by extoling in high terms, the nice sense of justice entertained by the British Government, and its scrupulous regard for the rights of nations.

Joseph Peabody, Esq., sworn. Is owner of the Brig Mexican. Shipped *ten* boxes of specie, containing two thousand dollars each. The boxes were marked P.—The brig sailed the 28th August, 1832. She arrived back in 42 days, being robbed of the specie. I have been engaged in the West India trade for *forty years.* I formerly sailed myself to and from the Havana. Passages vary from ten to thirty days. Vessels bound from Cuba to Africa do not steer a strait course across the Atlantic, but follow the Gulf Stream until they get as far north as Lat. 30 or 34. A fast sailing vessel leaving the Havanna on the 20th, and a dull sailing vessel leaving Salem on the 29th of the month would be likely to meet in the spot where the Mexican was robbed. The Bill of Lading, and Register produced in Court are the genuine ones.

Capt. John Groves Butman, sworn. I commanded the Brig Mexican. I sailed on the 29th Aug. 1832, and had twenty thousand dollars in specie on board, stowed down in the run. On the 20th Sept. lat. 33 lon. 34. 30 fell in with a schooner, she passed across our bow at 4 A. M., she was a Baltimore clipper, low, straight and long, at day-break she was on our weather quarter standing from us, after daylight she tacked and stood towards us, between 9 and 10 she was on our weather bow. The wind then shifted a little, we tacked ship because we did not like the appearance of the strange sail. We now perceived a man stationed in her foretop on the look-out, shortly after the schooner squared her sails and stood directly down upon us. When within gunshot she fired a gun to leeward, I now hove to, when a little to windward of us she hailed me. Her distance from us was 30 or 40 yards. I now saw two guns on deck and a large number of men, he asked where we were from, where bound, and what our cargo was on board, I answered our cargo was saltpetre and tea. I was now ordered on board, I took four of my men and went in the boat to her, when we got to her gangway they ordered me to come on board at the fore chains, when we got to the chains five of the schooner's crew jumped into our boat and ordered us back to the brig, none of my crew went on board the schooner. When we got back to the brig they all rushed on deck and ordered me down into the cabin, I went down and they followed me. As soon as I turned round two of them drew their knives on me and stabbed them at my throat, exclaiming, *Money, Money*, in broken English. I was now very much alarmed, and called the mate and crew to come down and get the money out from the run under the cabin floor.

They beat my crew with their knives to make them work quick. After the money was got up they insisted I had more, and pulled over all the chests, boxes, and berths, and told me if they found any they would cut my throat, I was now left alone in the cabin. Soon after as I attempted to go on deck, one of them drove me back and struck me with the speaking trumpet. Saw the boat going to the Panda, and return with 12 or 15 men. Heard them jump on board and close up the hatchways, soon after this heard a great noise as if the mainsail had fallen, soon after a spar was thrown on deck. We were now all fastened below, and half suffocated with smoke coming down from the camboose. From the cabin window we saw them return to the Panda. They carried one of our spars on board and sunk my boat, they now made sail. We now got on deck through the cabin sky-light, and found every thing in confusion. All the standing and running riggiug was cut away, the mainsail cut into ribbons and hanging over the camboose, the camboose burnt half up, in it was a tub of rope yarns, on fire, and other combustibles. In a few moments the fire would have reached the mainsail and set the masts on fire, all the sails were cut up badly. I cannot swear to the identity of any of the prisoners at the bar, I can swear that there was a man chained to one of the prisoners in Salem who drew his knife on me.

Cross Ex. I should say the schooner was 150 tons burden, the guns appeared to be 12 pounders. There was 50 or 60 men on board, could not swear there was a gun amidships.

Stephen Badlam. I saw Manuel Delgardo, the man identified by Capt. Butman. He cut his throat in the jail, with a bit of glass, I saw him after death.

Benjamin Brown Reed—I was first mate of the Mexican. In the morning when I came on deck to stand watch, about 4 o'clock, the second mate told me a vessel had passed astern of us about an hour before. Asked him to pass up the glass, took it and went on the forecastle. Saw her standing for us, went down and told the captain, I thought the vessel wanted to hail us. They were on the starboard tack, she appeared full of men, and manoeuvered in a suspicious manner. The captain now called me, and we consulted where the money should be put, I told him it was no use to do any

The Mate begging his Life.

thing with it as every one on board knew where it was, as they saw it taken on board in Salem harbour, and if we denied having it, and they should find it, we would only fare harder. While we were talking, the 2d mate came down and said they were chasing us, and had fired a gun. Ran on deck and saw the smoke of her gun. The captain ordered our brig to be hove to, and we hoisted American colors. The schooner now hailed us, there was a man on the foretop gallant yard, he was there from our first seeing the pirate in the morning, till we lost sight of her in the afternoon. I reached the manropes to them and saw the knives in their sleeves. We were now all called into the cabin. The Spaniards came up and threatened to cut our throats with their knives, they made us go down one at a time, and beat us to make us get the money out quick, they made such a flustration that it was sometime before we could do any thing. Two men got into the run to get the money out, but could not work for want of room, at last after great confusion the steward lifted up the boxes and we passed them on deck. They hailed the Panda and said there was plenty of money on board. The boatswain kicked me forward, and then kicked me down the forecastle, called me up, sent me down again, and placed a man over me as guard. I begged hard for my life, he asked me what o'clock it was, and before I could get it out, he snatched it from me, he demanded my money, sent a man to get it from the wood pile on deck where it had been hid before they boarded us. They asked for our chronometer, and struck the captain so hard with the speaking trumpet as to bend it all up, they drove us all down the hatchway and made all the hatches fast; we kept quiet till the pirate got to a great distance; when we got up through the cabin skylight, the camboose was all on fire. The mainsail soon would have caught, and the masts would soon have gone by the board, and we should have all been burnt up. Two of the men are now present who boarded the Mexican. *The witness now went and put his hand on Francisco Ruiz, and said,* "this is the man that was stationed at the forecastle to keep me down." *Manuel Boyga was the other. These two men now rose and with the fiercest gesticulations denied what the witness had asserted.* I saw another person at Salem who boarded us, he cut his throat in jail.

Cross Ex. The Capt. at first thought the men on board the Panda were the dead eyes of the lower rigging. We thought she was a pirate and tried to avoid her. The boatswain had a bunch on his nose, some of the Pirates shifted their clothes on board, putting on ours and leaving theirs. One of the Pirates had on cowhide shoes. The long knives were about a foot in length.

Benjamin Larkum. I shipped as boy on board the Mexican, I can recognize two of the prisoners at the bar. *The witness went and put his hand on Ruiz the piratical carpenter,* "I saw that man with the first boats' crew that came on board." I went in the boat with Capt. Butman on board the pirate. When we got back I stayed in the boat and bailed her out, I heard a great noise on board, was frightened and crept into the head. I thought they were murdering our crew, I was not frightened when the schooner first hailed us, but when I saw their knives in their sleeves when they boarded us, I was scared.

Cross Ex. I should think the pirate about 150 tons, I could see the figure head from the place where I concealed myself.

John Battis. I am 18 years old, I was with the Mexican. I can swear to the identity of two of the prisoners. *He went up and put his hand on Ruiz and Boyga. They rose with great indignation and exclaimed in the most savage manner,* "you lie, you say you saw us." I first recognized these men on board the Savage in Salem harbour.

Thomas Fuller. Was a seaman on board the Mexican. I think there is one person here whom I recognize to be one of the pirates that robbed us. *Fuller went up to identify Ruiz, and struck him a terrible blow, and then retreated back very suddenly. The prisoners all resented this with great indignation.*

The court reprimanded the witness for his uncourteous recognition. "I am not certain he is one, I think he is, I saw him beat the steward with an oak baton in the forecastle."

Cross Ex. Had no more enmity for him than the rest. Mr Dunlap now said to Fuller, if you had struck *lighter* your evidence would have been *harder*.

Benjamin Daniells. I can identify one person who boarded us, it is Ruiz the carpenter. *He put his hand on him in a gentle manner.* I am positive he was one who boarded us, he drove us around the vessel, I was much alarmed when they drew their knives on us.

Thomas C. H. Ridgely—Black Cook. When the pirates came on board the Mexican, I had a good chance to see them come in the gang way. I was lying my body over the camboose, had my feet on some spars. I saw *Antonio Ferrer*, the black man, on the fore top sail yard of the Panda, saw the scars on his face. The vessel sometimes came within a few feet of us, and then yawed off. *Antonio now rose and said, "you must have fine eyes to see that distance."*

John Lewis—Black Steward. This is the man that beat me down in the half deck with an oak baton, *putting his hand on Ruiz.* He beat me because I would not tell him where the money was.

Cross Ex. He broke the baton into three pieces in striking me. I lifted the money out of the run. *Mr Child to Lewis.* What have you and the cook been talking about since you have been confined in the same room. We have been talking about nothing. *(A Laugh.)*

Joseph Perez, one of the Panda's crew taken for a United States' Evidence.

Mr Dunlap requested Mr Badlam, the interpreter, to say to Perez—"You are now put to the bar as a witness; and if you tell the truth, the whole truth, and nothing but the truth, you will not be prosecuted."

Judge Story instructed Mr Badlam to repeat Mr Dunlap's proposition to Perez, by one sentence at a time, and to add "If you do not tell the truth, the whole truth, and nothing but the truth, you will be liable to be prosecuted as much as any other of the Pirates"—and to add the distinct question to him—"Are you willing to testify upon these conditions?"

This question being answered in the affirmative, a Bible,

certified by the Bishop to be such, was produced, and with his left hand on the New Testament portion of the Scriptures, and the right one raised, he was sworn according to the most solemn form known.

Judge Story then asked, through the interpreter—"Do you believe God will punish you, if you testify falsely?"

Perez answered affirmatively, and the examination proceeded; he testified as follows, with the exception of such omissions, as are not deemed essential:—

Joseph Perez. I was born in the island of Margueritta, in Colombia; am about 22 years old. I was taken to Havana in a vessel, a prisoner, and stayed there four months. Afterwards, about two years and four months ago, I joined the Panda at Havana; Pedro Gibert, now present, was her commander; Bernardo de Soto, present, was her mate; Francisco Ruiz, present, was her carpenter; *all* of the prisoners were of the crew, but all the crew are not here. When we sailed from Havana, there were 30 in all, including the officers. When we sailed from the mouth of the harbor, in passing Moro Castle we were hailed—"where bound?" We answered, to St. Thomas and Principi, on the coast of Africa, and our Captain's name given "Pedro Gibert." We sailed at 8 in the morning, somewhere about the 20th or 26th of August. We first spoke a corvette on the 20th of September, at 4 in the morning. I first saw the American brig, heading south; the Captain was asleep; it was the 2d mate's watch; the captain got up and ordered the schooner to be put about; we tacked ship and stood for the brig. When it began to be more light, the brig altered her course to west, with all sails set; our schooner then set all her sails. I was stationed in the foretop; at half past 6 I sung out, "A sail;" it was to windward of the American brig; I should call it a schooner brig. About 8, the Mexican altered her course and sailed south; the Panda loosened her sails and stood for the brig; a sailor on board went forward to the bows and fired a musket: the Mexican hove to, and hoisted an American flag: the Panda hoisted a Colombian flag. A sailor, who spoke English, hailed the brig, "Where do you come from?" "From Boston," was the answer.

The Town of Lopez on the River Nazareth. The Panda at Anchor.

A boat from the brig, with four men and an officer, rowed to our schooner—came on the larboard side.

The 3d mate, boatswain, carpenter and one sailor got into the brig's boat, and went to the brig—that is, *four* men of the Spanish schooner embarked in the boat for the American brig. There the carpenter sits [here arose a brief, but most ferocious gabbling between the witness and Ruiz, who appeared ready to fly at each other's throats]—the 3d mate ran away at Nazareth—the boatswain died at Fernando Po, a prisoner—Delgardo was the name of the sailor, and he died in Boston Jail. The people of the brig went below in the forecastle—the 3d mate took the speaking trumpet and sung out to the captain of our schooner: "There is on board what you wish; what you are looking for; she carries $20,000, as put down in the papers of the vessel; the money is in 10 boxes, containing $2000 each." The boatswain held up a handful of dollars and showed them to the captain, and afterwards threw them into the sea. The captain sung out, "Very well, very well; let her be well scorched, and let it all come on board."

The $20,000 were brought on board; it was money; I saw it with my own eyes from the top; the schooner's launch towed the American boat to the schooner. * * * I looked so intently at what was going on in the brig, that the captain scolded me, and sent another man up to look out; four men then went on board the brig; they were Garcia, Montenegro, Castillo, and Ruiz, [all in court]. I was in the tops; told the captain there was a sail in sight; "Where away?" said he, "Astern of the American brig." "How close?" "So nigh, I can see her 3 masts." At this time, one of my comrades in the American brig was standing guard over the forecastle, with a handspike; the captain sang out to take them [brig's crew] out of the forecastle, and shut them up in the cabin; the 3d mate, with a sword, and a sailor, with a knife, then chased them aft from the forecastle to the cabin; the people were shut below with a padlock. After they were all shut up below, saw smoke; they all then started for the schooner, bringing a keg of butter and one of lard; when about half way to the schooner, 3d mate and boatswain got out of the American boat and knocked her bottom out with something heavy; when our launch was hoisted, we turned a gun towards the brig, and made a round turn across her bows. * * *

The Panda first made Cape Monte, on the coast of Africa, then Port Bazaar, staid there some days, took in water, &c. one morning saw a frigate running down with all sails set—our captain then ordered all the knives to be taken away from the crew—the frigate saw us, and sailed on the other tack—our captain ordered us to weigh anchor, and with a light wind and oars we got out from Grand Bazaar—went to Cape Lopez—thence to the river Nazareth, in November, and left me ashore there to look after the slaves, the schooner sailed to the Isle of Principi, in January. When they came back from Principi, they came running away, and they ran the schooner ashore, on the beach of Cape Lopez—the captain came ashore at Nazareth—I was his servant, and while setting the table I heard him tell the boatswain that he had to fly from Principi because the news of the American brig robbery had reached there—he had bought $250 dollars' worth of provision, which he was obliged to leave, the schooner remained at Nazareth about 4 months,—when the English hove in sight with their boats, the carpenter went into the cabin, took up the after scuttle, and put a brimstone match to a bag or keg of powder—the rest of the crew had all gone ashore—the carpenter then left in a canoe. Before he left he took the papers of the schooner, and brought them with him. The captain and men all went to the negro barracks, and remained there till the English vessel went to sea.

The British brig took the schooner off to sea, but both came back again, and came to an anchor; the English commander came on shore, and demanded the captain, mate, and carpenter; captain hid himself in a negro hut; the commander demanded them of the black king; he refused to deliver them up; the captain of the brig began to fire on the town from the pivot gun of the schooner Panda, a 12 or 16

Burying the Money on the Beach at Cape Lopez.

pounder, till she caught fire during the bombardment. After the English went away, the money was hid in a barrel, on the beach, on the right side of the river; the captain that day gave orders to move back into the woods as the English boats were coming down upon us; we took the money to Cape Lopez, and buried it there; I went after it there again by the captain's orders, with Boyga, Castillo, Ruiz, and Velasquez; while Castillo and I were digging up the money, the others began to count it; I said there were too many musquitoes here to throw away time in counting the money; one of them replied, that it was the captain's orders to count it, and leave *five thousand dollars* there for him. After his $5,000 were left, there were about $6,000 which we took to the negro barracks. We divided this money between us. * * * We were sitting in a dark room; the carpenter and captain up stairs talking; the carpenter came down, and said, "The captain is going to divide the money, and if *all* did not go and get their share, there would be the devil to pay." They all then went and got their share. * * * * * * *

I delivered myself up at Fernando Po—myself, Castillo, Montenegro and Garcia, and Delgardo, went there together in a boat—was taken in an English transport to Ascension, Sierra Leon, back again to Fernando Po, then to Principi, back to Ascension, where I found the rest of the prisoners in custody. We five were taken to Plymouth, in England, in the merchant schooner Hope, and then put on board a 74—while on board of the 74, the other prisoners were also brought in by the British man-of-war brig Curlew, and put on board of the 74 with us, and we were all brought to this country in the 10 gun brig Savage.

Joseph Perez—[cros-ex.] The cargo of our schooner consisted of 60 pipes new rum—bales of clothing, 30 bundles, all sizes—some dry goods—pieces of cloth—250 muskets—powder—flints—boxes of swords and cutlasses—1 barrel knives—2 boxes axes—beads, necklaces—I shipped for $20 per month—able seamen had $25. * * * It is customary in all vessels going and returning from the coast ot Africa to have a man in the tops—the Panda was painted black with a white streak—billet head—before she left Nazareth, the billet head was taken off, and an awkward piece of wood put on—we made her a two topsail schooner—she left Havana a foretopsail schooner—3 or 4 days after the robbery she put up her maintopsail—we saw an hermaphrodite brig while we were robbing the Mexican—then a ship, which we ran away from—some of the sailors said she was a man-of-war—don't know whether she chased us or not, but she came nearer—saw the captain take a pistol, which came from the American brig, out of the third mate's hand, and throw it overboard—Captain Gibert said he did not want any such thing on board—wanted nothing but money. * * * The third mate had a sword—the sailors had knives ground sharp at the point, like daggers—it is customary to give the men jacknives, but the men themselves bring long knives in their bags. * * * *

That day the captain said to the men—"Boys, take off your hats and put on your caps, and change about." Those that were obedient took their hats off, and those that were not kept theirs on. * * * I cannot read Spanish, much less English—all the letters of the alphabet which I know is, P, D, O and U, [witness then explained that he meant *written* or Italian characters—he succeeded in making out nearly all the letters in print, and read a number of words correctly in the Spanish translation of the indictment.] I want to tell how I got $250—the boatswain 500—Delgardo 300—Montenegro 250, and the mate $2,400—he confessed his guilt in Sierra Leon, [at this point the witness spoke so fast that it was impossible to interpret, or take down his testimony—he was therefore repeatedly interrupted, till losing all patience, he exclaimed in English—"I will say, and by G—d I will"—and when checked again, misunderstood a remark, and drew the inference that he was rendering himself liable to the same punishment as the other prisoners, by what he was testifying. He in consequence became excited, and was made quite frantic by Capt. Gibert's remarking to him, that he took him on board of his schooner out of charity. The interpreters were requested to take him out and tranquilize him, by an explanation. When they returned, Judge Story requested the interpreters to assure him, if laboring under any delusion of danger, of his perfect safety. Mr. Child objected to any such intimation being given, but Mr. Dunlap moved that he be assured that the faith and honor of the government pledged to him by its legal officers, should be faithfully kept. Mr. Child replied, with great vehemence, to this motion, and concluding by saying—"I believe the unhappy men at this bar are totally innocent of the crime they are charged with—I believe them to be the victims of one of the foulest plots that was ever contrived." The assurance, however, was given, and the confidence of the witness being restored he proceeded

* * * There was nothing said about dividing the money till the English had taken the schooner. The captain had $4000 of the money in his trunk when he ran her

ashore. The captain brought a watch, valued at $400, and a shaving machine, worth $400, from Prince Isle—knew they were bought with the stolen money, because the vessel had not a quarter of a cent, when she left Havana—was captain's steward. * * * The negro interpreter took the money the captain had, at the time the English came to Nazareth, and hid it in his own yard—we buried $11,000 at Cape Lopez—don't recollect the day we dug it up again—left $5000 for the captain—does'nt recollect the day, because he was so afraid of being made a prisoner—had never been in such a dirty scrape before—we five that went to Fernando Po threw our money overboard, because the boatswain said it would be our own condemnation—when the captain called me to receive my share of the money, it was laying by his side on the floor—$250—he said, "You may want a little money to buy clothes, and you may go, as you have been wanting to go this long time." The captain had a knife in his bosom—I believe his intention was to kill any one who refused to take his share of the money—the boatswain had $500—Garcia $400—Castillo $250—Montenegro $250—Delgardo $300—the mate, De Soto, $2,400—the 3d mate ran away at Lopez, and the captain sent him $1000, by the carpenter—there was no rule agreed upon for dividing the money—the captain was the sole owner, and did as he had a mind to with it—he had one lot of $4000, and another of $5000—don't know what become of the rest. * * * When carpenter failed to blow up the schooner on the beach, captain asked why he did not spread powder on the deck, tie a string to the lock of the gun, and as he rowed ashore give it a slant, and thus fire it off among the powder on the deck, and so set fire to her—had purchased 60 slaves—the schooner was to carry 450 slaves. * * *

At Fernando Po, I denied that I belonged to the Panda at first, but when put under oath I confessed that I did belong to her—by advice of boatswain, we agreed to say we belonged to the Spanish brig Little Negro, which was cast away—the boatswain continued to say so, till confronted by a Portuguese, who had seen him on board of the

Panda, when he owned it, when examined there I was put into a room by myself—Delgardo also confessed—the Governor made him sign a paper—they never offered me anything—it was my own fear that made me declare—they said if I lied, and it turned out that I belonged to the Panda, I should be hung—my heart failed me, and I told the whole story. They had a newspaper there containing an account of the robbery of the Mexican. When I spoke of the $20,000, one of the clerks took up the paper, and said "True," and threw it down on the table.

The Pirates concealed in the Woods behind Cape Lopez.

I did not come here bribed.—I did not say, when I saw the boatswain dead at Fernando Po, "God forgive me for bearing false witness against him." * * * On board the Victoria, 74, at Plymouth, the captain and mate told me to say I knew no English, and to deny every thing. Captain conversed with all the prisoners. I told the Cook, Ferrer, that the Captain wanted all of them to deny everything, so that he himself might turn king's evidence, and that the captain had offered to,—the captain and mate have tried several times to get me to deny every thing. * * Perico was the name of the sailor who hailed the Mexican in English—they say he died when the schooner went to Principi. * * I was on board of a Spanish schooner when Morillo commanded the Spanish forces, but I don't know how old I was. [This answer was given to a question that was propounded to him, in a variety of forms, and he broke out—"I don't want to be bothered with these questions in this way—I know they come from the prisoners."] I was taken into Havana in the brig Eagle a prisoner,—I was cabin boy of her,—we were taken because we had slaves on board. Costa was on board the Eagle.—Costa was cabin boy on board the Panda,—heard Costa say that Ferrer was a slave. I did not know when I shipped that there was any intention of robbery—all vessels bound to the coast of Africa have to report their crew to the general of marine, but our crew was not inspected by him—I don't know the reason why our crew did not go to his office—I did not know the captain then; if I had, I should sooner have stopped ashore, and ate dirt, than have gone with him—saw the carpenter give the captain the schooner's papers, in the barracoon [negro barracks], but don't know what became of them after—the schooner sailed from Havana under a Spanish flag. Before we robbed the Mexican we robbed an English vessel; hailed the English corvette, and asked if they could sell us a topmast, as our main topmast was not up; then asked the captain to come on board, but the English answered that his boat leaked. The third mate, boatswain, &c. went on board of the English vessel; the third mate hailed the schooner, and said that there was *not* on board *what* he wanted; they took some leather; lemons, cordials, rigging, a spyglass, cabin curtains, and monkey jackets.

One of the Boxes of Dollars.

The crew obeyed every command of the captain, and

after the robbery of the Mexican, the captain was still *greater* and *greater*. We had been out about 8 days.

We did not commit any other robbery after robbing the Mexican; but at Sesto the captain wanted to sink a Spanish schooner laying there—he got the gun all ready, and fixed the tackle to the anchor to weigh it, but the sea was too heavy and he gave it up.

In answer to the question—"Have you ever received any money since you were taken?" Perez replied; you are trying to do with me what the Spanish consul tried to do in England; trying to make me confess that I was bribed.

Mr. Child. Have you ever confessed that you were drunk when you gave your declaration at Fernando Po?

Perez. The scoundrel that says so is a liar.

In answer to Mr. Dunlap,—the papers brought ashore from the schooner by the carpenter and given to the captain, were put in a tin box, all wet. In the negro barracks, when the English brig was in sight, I heard De Soto say to the third mate, that he had been up all night making up a false log book, so as to make it appear, that the schooner came a different way than she did come. I went to school eight months; they tried to make me read printed letters; I can read print a little, but can neither write nor read writing. The 3d mate, who I saw at the negro hut after he left, gave as a reason for running away that news of the robbery of the Mexican had reached Principi.

Anastasio Silvera.—I was born at St. Catherine, in the Brazils; am 23 years old; I belonged to the Panda; I joined her at Princes Island, on the 9th of February, 1833; Don Pedro Gibert was captain, and De Soto was mate [witness indentifies all the prisoners as belonging to the crew of the Panda]; I went on board at nine in the morning, and the schooner sailed in half an hour after; went to Cape Lopez, and thence to the river Nazareth; the river is 4 or 6 leagues from Lopez; she ran ashore at Lopez, and the carpenter said he was going to set her on fire; the captain sent me and the other Portuguese taken on board at Princes Island ashore; they got her off again; I did not go up the river with her; the captain sent me on board after she got up the river; at Nazareth the captain and mate lived ashore in a barracoon—8 or 9 of the crew lived on board; the rest lived on shore; the cargo we were going to take were slaves; when the English boats came into the river on the 4th of June, the carpenter told us to jump into the boat and go ashore, as he was going to set fire to the schooner; but the carpenter came on shore without setting her on fire, whether through fear because the English boats were so near, or not, I do not know; the carpenter was the last man on board, he came on shore in a canoe after the crew left in the boat; I went to the barracoon where the captain was, at Nazareth town; I staid there one day, when the captain turned me and the rest of the Portuguese away, and said it was because he had nothing to support us with; I went to a negro house and staid 9 or 10 days; the Panda went out of the river, but came back in 10 or 15 days; there was a Portuguese schooner laying there; I asked the captain of her if he would give me a passage to Princes Island, and he said he would. The English captain was on board of the Portuguese schooner, at this time, and pressed me, and I was taken on board of the Panda, a prisoner; the next day the English commenced firing on the town from the Panda, and upon firing the second gun she blew up; they put me and the rest of the Portuguese on board of a little Portuguese sloop that lay there, from which I was taken on board the Curlew; Domingo and I, when we first left the Panda, went back in the country together, but on the same day he left me and said he was going back to the Panda, but I don't know whether he did go on board of her or not, as I did not see him after.

Cross-examined. Before I joined the Panda, I had been at Princes Island a month and a half, on board of a Brazilian brig—the brig had been there, I think, over fifteen days—I did not see her till two or three days after she had been there—it was in the month of January, but what day I don't know—the captain of the Panda was to give me $120 for the voyage round to Nazareth and back to Havana—one of the others shipped for the same wages—she was a two-topsail schooner, had a bray pivot-gun, and two carronades—the head was neither a fiddle-head nor a billet-head—it was long and slim, and turned up at the end—the main topsail yards were smaller than the fore yards—had twelve men on board when I first went on board—afterwards I saw seven more at the barracoon [see testimony of Perez]—the custom-house boat was along side, when I went on board, but I do not know that the custom-house officers overhauled her—I think Ferrara, the Governor of the Island, was the consignee of the Panda's cargo—I heard that the mate was sick at the Governor's house—I heard no report of the piracy of the Mexican at Princess Island—I never saw any money on board—we were not chased while going to Lopez—saw no vessel while going from Princes Island to Lopez.

When we were going to leeward of the Cape Lopez, the

Explosion of the Panda.

schooner touched, or dragged on the bottom; we passed one gun forward, and got her off into deep water and anchored—remained two days; the captain then said she was unseaworthy, and not fit to make the voyage to Havana, and must be ran ashore, and set fire to—and he gave that as a reason for weighing anchor, and going up the river so quick; when she got to Nazareth the mate said there was 4 feet of water in her; saw no money taken out of her at the time she was anchored off Cape Lopez—muskets, pistols, swords, beef, bottles of gin, &c. were taken out. She lay about a gun shot to the leeward of Cape Lopez—I am certain that she ran ashore; I was on board and ran a line ashore; at Nazareth I was kept ashore to take care of the slaves; lead them to bathe, and

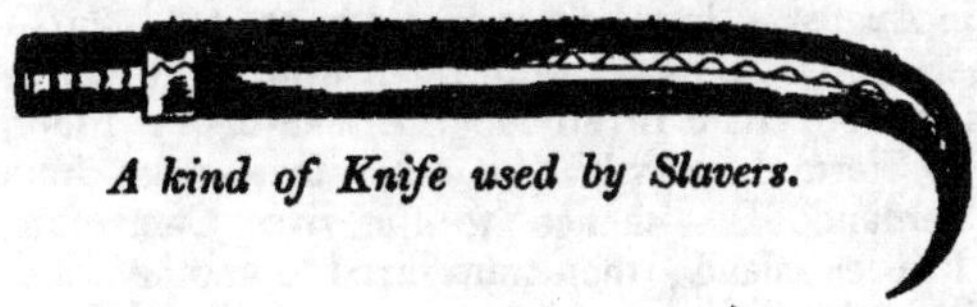

A kind of Knife used by Slavers.

give them water and victuals; the 3d mate went away in an English hermaphrodite brig, in February or March—the day the third mate went ashore, he and the boatswain had a quarrel, in which the boatswain received a small wound—I don't know where—I do not know that the 3d mate went away because he had wounded the boatswain; I don't know what trade the English brig was engaged in—nor where she went.

The prisoners all told me that they abandoned their cargo to trade in slaves—[the witness describes the attack on the Panda, and escape of her crew, precisely as other witnesses]—one or two muskets were fired from the English boats, [Mr. Child here contradicts Mr. Peyton's interpretation, but Mr. Tavers, the native Portuguese, confirms Mr. Peyton]—I can only swear that they fired one, two, or three—they were very near when we first saw them—the schooner lay at anchor in a bite or cove—the English did not open a fire as soon as they got round the point, but pulled directly for the schooner, with an English flag—as soon as they got on board of the schooner they fired a gun, and another in the evening, but I don't know what for—I don't know of any money having been buried by any of the crew of the Panda—[interpretation challenged by Mr. Child, and Mr. Peyton was sustained by Mr. Tavers, in his interpretation]—I don't know whether the English searched for money or not—I don't know where the captain of the Panda was taken prisoner—sailed from river Bonney to Fernando Po, where the Captain of the Curlew heard that there were five of the Panda's crew there—I went ashore there—remained 34 or 35 days; I never went on board of the Curlew again—I went, with Montenegro, Garcia, and Castillo, now here, and Perez and Delgardo not here, to Ascension, in an English transport.

It was in August I left Fernando Po in the transport—arrived there about 30 days before the Curlew—at Ascension I was put on board of an English man-of-war *Flora*, and went to Sierra Leon with the other five—went from there to Fernando Po—thence to the river Camarone; thence to Princes Island; then transferred to another English brig Trinado, and went back to Ascension, and found the Curlew there; then put on board of the Esperanza, and went to England; don't recollect the length of the voyage; touched at St. Michael's; stopped two days; thinks the voyage lasted 60 days; I did not see the other prisoners at Ascension; only the five; I was always a prisoner; I was always the first that they put in irons, when we were ironed; we were all called up and put to work in the day time; to wash deck, sheet home, or set the sails, or clew them up; on board of the Curlew, we were two or three days in irons; when first taken into the other vessel, slept the first night in irons; when we got to sea the irons were taken off; at Ascension we were kept four days in jail ashore, in irons; at Sierra Leon, we were kept ashore two days, taking *declarations*, (i. e. depositions;) at St. Michael's we slept in the forecastle with a sentry over us; when we arrived in England, we were not put in chains.

I never heard Perez [United States' evidence, already examined,] say any thing about the testimony he had given or was to give in this case—never heard any one talk to Perez about it—whenever I saw Perez talking, I always cleared out—I did not like his conversation—he always spoke blackguard about my father and mother—*mocha palavara*—the whole of them would blackguard one another about each other's fathers and mothers. [Mr. Peyton here explains that among Spaniards, when they get angry with each other, they always abuse each other's parents.] I heard Perez say, in the presence of some of these prisoners, that they had robbed the American brig—and they at that time owned it; Perez also said that the declarations he had made at Fernando Po he would always stick to.

Perez said he confessed because it was the truth, and the other prisoners said it was true; they said so more than twenty times on board of the Esperanza, on her way to England; the first time I heard of the robbery of the Mexican was on board of the Panda, after she was captured; I learnt it from one of the Portuguese who shipped with me; he said the carpenter told him; at Fernando Po, they all five wanted to confess, but made such a noise that they would not let them; a great many things that Perez would say, they would say was true, and at other things he would say, they would cry out it was a lie; they would get mad with each other during the examination, and call each other rascals; no promises made to them to induce them to confess; would not even give me a shirt; if it had not been for the goodness of the English sailors, I should not have had any thing to cover my flesh; no threats were made; no musket ever pointed at the black man, to my knowledge; at Fernando Po, in the Governor's house, he asked the whole of the five if they had robbed the Mexican; they said they had; the English captain was present; the first day they denied it.

When the English captain came on shore at the river Nazareth, I saw the Captain and crew of the Panda go back into the forest which borders on the town—the captain went one way and the crew another; I never knew

Captain Trotter to give wine or rum to Perez; I never heard Perez say that what he had confessed [told] about the piracy was all a lie; I never heard Perez say to the prisoners: "*I would rather take your lot than mine.*" We Portuguese all told Captain Trotter that we shipped in Princes Island, in reply to him, when he asked us if we came from Havana in the Panda. I don't know why the Esperanza was captured; her boatswain, cook, and a negro were taken to England. The English talked about sending them to this country, but the Portuguese consul interfered and prevented it; I don't know what became of them; I was present when the boatswain of the Panda died at Fernando Po; I never heard Perez say any thing about him after his death; I have not conversed with any one about this matter since I came to America; I do not know that several of the prisoners have had offers of liberty if they would testify against the rest of the crew; I don't know that any of them have had offers of clothing and a conveyance to their own country if they would testify; I feel quite certain that I have had no conversation about these matters with other persons than the prisoners, either here or in England, except with the Spanish Consul in this city; he asked me something about the death of the boatswain.

George H. Quentin—I am an officer in the British navy, I am a master's assistant [i. e. midshipman]—came to Salem in the 10 gun brig Savage, on the 27th of August, direct from Portsmouth, England—the prisoner's were received on board at Spithead. I was attached to the brig Curlew, commanded by Henry Dundas Trotter; I. belonged to her about 3 years and a half; had been at Cape of Good Hope; arrived on the coast of Africa in January, 1833; touched at Princes Isle in March; in May, at Princes Isle, we received information that a piracy had been commited on the Mexican, and that a vessel, answering the description, contained in the Salem Gazette, of the pirate schooner, was laying in the river Nazareth.

We then sailed for the river Nazareth, and arrived there on the 4th of June; three of our boats, armed, went up the river with about forty men; Capt. Trotter himself commanded the boats; I was in one of them: just after daylight, we observed the schooner laying at anchor; we pulled up, but kept out of sight as much as possible: when we got within a mile of her, we hoisted a "union jack;" we were at that moment behind a point of land. A soon as we hove in sight of the schooner, her whole crew left her, except one man, and we soon saw him go off in a canoe. Capt. Trotter then chased the canoe, but could not come up with her, and returned to the schooner. I was the first who boarded the schooner; there was not a soul on board; saw nothing but smoke issuing from the cabin; one man went down, and found a slow match, made of brimstone and cotton, burning in the magazine, where there were fourteen or sixteen quarter casks of powder; it was hauled from the cabin burning; the fire was immediately put out with water; the hatch was off the magazine. The captain gave orders to look for the schooner's papers and log-book and all other papers: one of the men found a few notes in the cabin; I searched, but found no papers; none were found:

Inhabitants of the Island of Fernando Po, in the Gulf of Guinea.

the notes were taken possession of by Capt. Trotter. We bent the sails of the schooner, and went down the river with her; had her in our possession ten or eleven days. She was a long, two-topsail schooner, figure-head cut off; raking masts, sharp like a Baltimore clipper, no name on her stern, had a slave deck, grated hatchway.

On the 6th day we went to Lopez; three days after the schooner blew up, killing 2 officers and 2 men; we supposed a spark from the gun fell into the magazine; we went to Lopez in search of the pirate-crew; we obtained Simon Domingo, a Portuguese, before we came down the river; the natives brought him off in a canoe, the same day; four other Portuguese were taken from the schooner Esperanza, but I don't know at what time; Silvera, the Portuguese, was picked up at Lopez. Captain Trotter sent a boat to demand the pirate captain and crew, and the king promised to give them up. The next morning I was sent ashore for them, and the king's son came down and said, "The men would be brought down as soon as the son had gone to dinner," meaning at 12 o'clock; they were not brought down.

In August we went to Fernando Po, and found five of the pirate's crew there; saw Perez there;—again to Lopez; I went in the Esperanza, a schooner we had taken; we obtained there Don Pedro, the captain, Ferrer, the black cook, Costa, the boy, and Joseph Velasquez; an English bark, trading there, who had some of our men on board, captured them. At St. Thomas's Island, we took De Soto, the mate, Ruiz, the carpenter, Boyga, and another; all were first put on board of the Curlew, but five went to England in the Esperanza, and the rest in the Curlew; all taken to Plymouth first, thence to Portsmouth, and thence to America.

Cross-ex.—The Esperanza taken because she was suspected of aiding and abetting the Panda, by giving a passage to her crew and their money. I found on board of the Panda a United States ensign and pennant—2 Spanish ensigns, 1 French ensign, and a Danish or Portuguese—she had a great quantity of round shot on board, besides cannister and chain shot—there were also double-headed shot, and grape, I never saw chain shot or grape shot on board of a trader on the coast of Africa before. There was a musket or two fired at the canoe with the carpenter in it, when leaving the schooner—the fire was not returned—I do not know that the crew of the Panda ever carried on hostilities against the

English—there was some firing on shore among the black fellows, but I do not know that any of our men were there, we never fired among the negro canoes—I am sure the pivot gun was not fired among them—none of our men were ever flogged for firing at the canoes, three or four days after the capture some of them were flogged for drunkenness and insolence to the commander—there were nine casks of rum in the hold of the Panda, and they broached one and got drunk—when the Panda blew up I was a mile and a half from her, going to the brig; a small trading Portuguese schooner rendered assistance; I do not know that any of the Panda's crew assisted in saving the lives of any of our people that were blown into the river. I am *sure—certain*, that the Panda's figure-head was cut off; I went to the bows to see; it was cut off smooth like the stern of a boat, I think there was a Spanish consul at Plymouth; a gentleman came on board there, who was said to be the consul; only saw him about five minutes; captain Trotter was sick with a fever several times on the homeward voyage; I have no knowledge that Capt. Gibert ever gave Capt. Trotter a Protest; the letters B. S. and some other initials were on the diamond ring taken from the mate; I do not know that the other letters stood for his wife's name; there was hair in it; I was not present when Capt. Trotter took the mate's watch from him: our orders were to cruize on the coast of Africa till further orders; we were retarded in waiting for orders; as soon as they were received, I did not perceive but what Capt. Trotter availed himself of every wind and circumstance to reach England.

Simon Domingo, one of the Panda's crew, who joined her on the coast of Africa. I was on the coast of Africa between two and three years ago—went from Brazil to Princes Island in the Portuguese schooner Harriet—while at Princes Island, I shipped in a Portuguese brig, and went to Bahia—I returned to Princes Island in another brig—I left her in Princes Island, and Capt. Pedro Gibert asked me if I would ship on board of his schooner Panda—Don Pedro Gibert was her commander—Bernardo de Soto was mate, Ruiz was carpenter—Antonio Ferrer was cook, all the rest of the prisoners here belonged to her crew then—it was on the 9th of February, 1833—we went to the river Nazareth, there dropped two anchors and moored her—bent the sails and sent down the maintopsail yard, she lay there four months—the Captain and officers went ashore, were engaged in buying slaves—I was taken prisoner, because I had said the Panda had robbed an American brig; four English boats came on board of the Panda; the carpenter set her on fire, and all the crew jumped into a boat and went ashore; I don't know how he set her on fire; I saw him run to the galley with a bag of powder, and I was scared, and got into the boat; the same day I went on board the Panda again; the English had possession of her, I heard from all the prisoners here that the Panda came from Havana.

Cross-ex. I was born on the Cape de Verds; I heard some of the crew confess to the captain of the English brig that they had robbed the Mexican; they had a Portuguese for an interpreter; they were the first five that were captured; Domingo Guzman confessed; he is a South American Indian, and as I knew some Indian, I interpreted for him; at

Bernardo de Soto. Don Pedro Gibert.

Fernando Po, before a Justice, Montenegro, Garcia, Castillo, Perez, Delgardo, and the boatswain confessed; they did not have the same names then that they have now; they were all sworn.

Mr Childs. During the four months you were laying in the river Nazareth before the capture of the Panda, did you ever hear the crew of the Panda say any thing about the robbery of the Mexican.

Mr Dunlap. I object to that question; it is an improper one; it is dangerous to the prisoners; for if answered in the negative it amounts to nothing, but if answered in the affirmative, it must be fatal to them.

Mr Childs. I am not afraid of the answer.

Mr Dunlap then withdrew his objection, and the witness proceeded.

I never heard them say any thing about it then; the English captain sent me with an officer and Velasques and the cook to look for the money, they took us to the place where the money had been buried, but it was gone; we then went into the forest to look for it; we did not look in the town for it. When the Spanish captain was taken at Cape Lopez, the English captain obtained some of the money, but I dont know how much it was; it was in a small bag. I never received any of that money from the English captain; I never received any money from him but one dollar for bread money, as I had been on short allowance.

Mr Child. Did not the English captain call all the crew up on deck, one by one, and give them some of the money taken from the captain of the Panda; and did you get some then?

Domingo. No, he did not. Before Gibert's money came on board, the captain said that to those who did not take any bread, he would at the end of the month, give the value of the bread in money. * * * When Captain Trotter went to demand the pirate crew, they went back into the woods, and the negroes formed on the beach armed; the negroes were not excited against the English, but only informed them that the pirates had gone back into the country. They did not keep the captain in irons, but when they came to a port to take in provisions, they put him in irons. After the first day I was taken out of irons to wait on the others who were in irons. * * * There were no presents offered to the five who confessed, nor were there any threats used to make them confess. * * * Bernardo de Soto went from the river Nazareth to St. Thomas, in the Esperanza, to purchase another vessel; and that was the reason she was captured.

George Budd, Esq. A Captain in the U. S. Navy.—I have been in the navy 29 years. Have commanded vessels in the West India station—have been to the Havana—vessels bound from Havana to Africa come as far north 31 or 35 deg. lat. A Baltimore clipper leaving Havana on the 20th and a merchant vessel leaving Salem on the 29th, would be likely to meet about the time and spot on which the Mexican was robbed. The route is the common thoroughfare to Africa. I have crossed the Atlantic in a clipper in 12 days. These kind of vessels are not so common as they were 18 years ago. They are used chiefly for illicit purposes. They carry very little cargo, and sail at a great expense, so they are unprofitable to owners unless engaged in a contraband trade. Our ships of war generally sail ten knots at most an hour.

Captain Joseph V. Bacon. I have been acquainted with nautical affairs 30 years, I have generally been engaged in the trade between Boston and Havana, Matanzas, &c. The winds that prevail in the Atlantic Ocean in the months of August and September, are generally from the west and south-west. A vessel from the Havana usually gets through the Bahama channel in four or five days.

Zachariah Jellison. I have made ten passages to the West Indies. I went as passenger—am acquainted with the navigation of those seas—I have made the passage from Salem to the Havana. There is a great probability of two vessels of the description of the Mexican and Panda meeting in the latitude and longitude marked out.

William H. Peyton (interpreter sworn as a witness)—I was once mate of a Spanish brig 4 years; her tonnage in Spanish measure was *ninety-five* tons; but when she was measured in Charleston, she was declared to be *one hundred and twenty* tons; I have been three voyages to Africa from Havana; on the first voyage I was quarter-master, on the second, 2d mate, and on the 3d, I was mate; have been in service since 1819—I think it is likely that vessels sailing in the latter part of August from Salem and Havana would fall in with each other in latitude 32 N. and longitude 37 W. if they fell in at all—I mean about that latitude and longitude; that is, they would be in the same region of the ocean. [Mr. Child, after this answer was given, objected to the question which drew it out, and said he did "not want Mr. Dunlap to play the part of cloud-compelling Jupiter, but wished to have the *clouds* of testimony gather naturally."] The farthest North we ever went was latitude 32—the ordinary passage is eight days, to get out from the Bahamas—I should shape my course to the eastward, to keep clear of the trade winds, and get into the variable winds, to bring up my *northing*.

[Mr. Peyton was subjected to a long cross-examination respecting the length of various voyages, and parts of voyages, to different ports in Africa; but as it related almost entirely to a portion of the ocean which the Panda could only have traversed in her last voyage, subsequent to the robbery of the Mexican, we cannot perceive that it can have much, if any, bearing on the case, at bar. Mr. Peyton stated that the natives of several ports in Africa will take dollars in payment of articles, but they are not current among themselves, and they only use them in making purchases of traders to their ports.]

I was five months a prisoner on the Island of Ascension. I was in Havana from June last till December—I saw the Panda there, anchored in the man-of-war grounds—she laid a mile from the town from which I saw her—she was rigged as a two top-sail schooner then, Baltimore clipper built, masts raked off about fifteen or twenty degrees, very low, appeared to be very deeply laden — it was in August that I saw her—the cargo of an African trader from Havana, so far as I know, is rum, tobacco, dry goods, muskets, pistols, powder, flints, cutlasses, Spanish dollars, &c.

When a captain of a merchantman is fitting out a vessel in the Havana, he obtains a number of sailors to work on board of her for a dollar a day and found; the day before she clears, the boatswain generally picks out the smartest for the crew; the next day they sign the papers; they then go to the office of the general of Marine, and are reviewed,

Ruiz leaving the Panda after applying the Slow Match.

and their licenses are examined; Spanish sailors are obliged to serve three years on board of a man of war, and when that term is out they receive a license to go where they please for the following three years. Their licenses are always examined before they can clear, to see if their term of liberty has expired; if it has expired, or is about expiring, they are sent on board of a man-of-war; if it has not expired, they are permitted to sail in the merchantmen. The first voyage I went, the sailor's wages were from 30 to 35 dollars per month; on my second voyage, from 40 to 45 dollars, but on my last only 20 to 25 dollars. It is usual for all African traders to take out money. I never knew but one vessel to go out without money, but she was overhauled and brought back, and the boxes marked money were found to contain nothing but brickbats. * * * I never heard Perez threaten the prisoners when he came into court. When he was raving, the prisoners jumped up, and said to him—"You'll be fixed yet," and shaking their fingers at him; he replied, you'll be fixed." That is the only time he said any thing like a threat.

Mr. Badlam then commenced reading the ship's papers; the first was a "royal passport," dated 29th of April 1831, permitting Captain Pedro Gibert to take a cargo of *lawful* merchandise direct to St. Thomas and Princes Island, the owners of the ship "to be made manifest to Capt. Gibert, and all other vassals of mine," signed "I, the King." The captain is expressly notified, in a note attached to this passport, that the vessel must not be employed to trade in *new* negroes, otherwise called *raw* negroes,—that is negroes not taught.

Paper 2. Moro Passport, dated Havana, August 18, granting a passport to make this particular voyage, in which the captain is called a Catalonian, and the mate a Corcican, and the whole crew, to the number of 30 enumerated. This pass winds up with a long chapter of wholesome marine morality. On the back of it is written, of the Panda, "she carries, solely for the defence of the vessel, one brass pivot gun, of 16; 2 gunnades of 12, in her battery, 24 muskets, 32 swords, 4 pairs of pistols, and corresponding munitions."

Paper 3. Bill of sale of the Panda, of 98 Spanish tons, dated August 7, 1832, to Bernardo de Soto, for $54,000, signed by Joseph Benedict Pardo, the former owner.

Paper 4—Invoice of cargo, a very full and choice one, precisely suited for the African trade.

Paper 6—Contract between the captain and owners; the captain's wages to be $100 per month, and 10 per cent. on the cargo, and $3, a head for every slave he brings.

Paper 7—Instructions to Capt. Gibert, to act according to his discretion, after consulting with his mate Bernardo de Soto, and to use due diligence, upon reaching his port of destination, to procure a return cargo: and to see that "*meekness and tenderness be observed on board,*" and to "*avoid all suspicious looking vessels.*" On his return, he is instructed "to enter Matanzas at night in silence, and, if hailed, say that you are from St. Thomas, *in ballast,*" and that there are certain officers there, who are advised of their wishes, and will instruct him what is proper for him to do.

When the reading of these papers was concluded, Mr Dunlap announced to the court, that the testimony in behalf of the Government had all been introduced. The examination of witnesses for the offence was then commenced, by calling to the stand *Juan B. Aranza*, captain of the Spanish merchantman Conda de Villaneuva, laying in this port; he was examined at great length, by Mr Child, upon routes, of voyages, rates of sailing, and distances of ports, and the general usages of the African trade. He confirmed, in the main, the government witnesses respecting the route from Havana to the coast of Africa, making no other variance than what might be naturally occasioned by the prevalence of different winds.

This witness testified that Captain Gibert bore a high character in Havana. Mr. Dunlap then asked the witness what he himself traded in, when on the African coast, and he replied "sometimes in *black ivory;*" but, being more closely pressed to explain what he meant by "black ivory," he admitted, that when he could not get a cargo of real ivory, he took one of slaves.

Santiago Elonzo—I have been an officer 3 years; have made voyages to Africa from Cadiz and Havana, have sailed in a clipper, clippers sail faster than other vessels, for they are built for nothing else but sailing, and not to carry cargoes—I can get *eleven and a half* knots out of a clipper with the same wind that I can only get *six* with, in my present brig.

Judge Story. Suppose a vessel sailed from Salem for Rio Janeiro on the 29th of August, and the schooner Panda sailed from Havana for Africa on the 20th, would they be likely to meet, or not?

Witness. I think it hardly possible for them to meet, as the schooner must get ahead of the brig; for I once knew a clipper to reach the Cape de Verds in 30 days. A brig from Salem, for Rio Janei o, would cross the Equator from 21 to 28 West, and the schooner would be in 12, at the same time. [The witness has been in the slave trade; and was a custom house officer in Havana four years.] I was acquainted with Captain Gibert, and he bears a very good character in the best mercantile houses in Havana.—When I was clerk in the custom house, in Havana, in 1827, I know that Capt. Gibert was a member of a mercantile house—he used to enter goods consigned to the house—the merchandise in their store was worth $10,000—I am not much acquainted with Bernardo de Soto, but have always heard merchants, concerned in the African trade, speak highly of him, he owned a schooner—afterwards purchased the Panda, and went out in her—the Panda once arrived at Havana with 420 slaves. In reply to a question, by Mr Dunlap, the witness says it was in the slave trade in which Bernardo de Soto gave satisfaction to the merchants.

Joseph Smith—I have been 25 years in the United States Navy, besides being in the merchant service before.—was 5 years a midshipman—14 years a lieutenant, and a master commandant ever since. [Having ascertained the rate of sailing of the Mexican, Captain Smith is of opinion, that the Panda would beat her 25 per cent.] It is not at all impossible, but only improbable, that the Mexican, sailing from Salem on the 29th, and the Panda from Havana on the 20th, would meet, provided that both vessels improved their time to the best advantage. [Mr Peyton was here called by Mr Child, to say whether a vessel could go to Cape Mount, in Africa, in 14 days, from lat. 33, long. 34.30, where the Mexican was robbed;—Mr Peyton was of opinion that she could not go in less than 28 or 30 days. Perez testified that the Panda made Cape Mount in 14 days after the robbery.] In reply to Mr Dunlap—If the brig and schooner would meet at all, it would be where the brig was robbed.

Capt. Beethold—A vessel bound to Rio from Salem, and one from Havana to Cape Mount, would probably meet where the brig and schooner met—the distance from Havana being enough greater to make up for the greater speed of the schooner.

In reply to Mr Dunlap—If the schooner made all possible speed, she might get a little further to the eastward [than lon. 34]—but if she did not take every advantage in her power, she might not get quite so far east; but my general opinion is, that they would meet about there, as that is the general thoroughfare.

Capt. Faucon—Been to sea 12 years—is master of a vessel, never sailed in a sharp vessel—have understood that the speed of such vessels is about 30 per cent. faster than other vessels. Supposing that the brig and schooner, sailing according to dates stated, took advantage of every thing, it would be *improbable*, but not *impossible* for them to meet.

Samuel Austin Turner—Have been six years in the U. S. Navy—is acquainted with the brig Mexican, the schooner would sail 9 knots, with the same winds that would carry the Mexican only 6, but in a *fresh* breeze, in which the Mexican would go *eight* knots, the schooner would exceed her only about *one* knot. From some calculations which I have made, the Mexican and Panda, under given data, would not approach each other nearer than one hundred miles—that is, taking it for granted, that they both avail themselves of every advantage.

Natives carrying two of the Pirates up the River Nazareth.

W. S. Bruce is somewhat acquainted with *Bernardo de Soto*. Has resided several years in the Havana, and his knowledge of the prisoner commenced in the fall of '31. De Soto was then the captain of the Spanish brig *Leon*, from Philadelphia to Havana. During one of his voyages from Philadelphia to the latter place, he saved and brought in the crew and passengers of the American ship, *Minerva*, which had taken fire. The passengers were thirty or forty in number, (chiefly Irish,) going to New Orleans or Mobile. De Soto's conduct was very highly spoken of at the time in Havana, and he was presented with a piece of plate by the merchants of New Orleans. Don't know that any one has asked him (De Soto) to become a witness against the rest of the prisoners. District Attorney did not request me to go to him. Did not intimate to me his wish or willingness that de Soto should be a witness. Should not have conjectured any thing of the kind from the District Attorney's conversation. Formed my opinion of the District Attorney's wishes from what was told me by a third person. That person was Charles W. Story. *I* told *de Soto* that he had better become a witness.

Mr. Dunlap. Had you ever conversed with me before you saw de Soto?

Witness. Yes, both before and afterwards.

Mr D. Recollect yourself.

Witness. You did not say any thing particular the first time.

Mr. D. Did you *ever* converse with me more than once?

Witness. No.

Mr. D. Did you not upon that occasion state to me what had passed between yourself and de Soto?

Witness. Yes.

Mr. D. Then, of course, sir, you never conversed with me before you saw de Soto.

In reply to a question from Mr. *Hillard* as to the state of public opinion in Havana in relation to persons engaged in the slave trade, the witness said that the being so engaged was not considered to disparage any man's character.

The Pirates carrying Rum on Shore to purchase Slaves.

Stephen Badlam. Has had a conversation with *Joseph Perez,* the government witness. About the 1st of October last was requested by the District Attorney to accompany him to the gaol for the purpose of interpreting between him and the prisoners. Witness and the District Attorney went into a room under the court, and directed the turnkey to bring in *Perez.* This was done, and witness then stated to the prisoner that the gentleman present, Mr. Dunlap, was the Attorney for the District, and had called, as the time of trial was approaching, to have some conversation with him. When I told *Perez* this, continued Mr. Badlam, he declared "that all he had previously said was false; that he had had a good deal of wine given to him, and had been told that if he became a witness he would not be considered in the light of the other prisoners, but be kept as a witness." He by this time appeared much out of humor, and said rapidly, as if in a passion, "I will not be a witness any longer, but will take my chance with the others." I think he also said, "that the English had deceived him, by telling him that he would not be kept a prisoner, while in reality he was now as much a prisoner as the others." I think when he said *this* he did not refer to any individuals in this country, but to the English. I cannot swear that he mentioned the English, but it is my impression that he did so. I have no doubt myself upon this point. I told Mr. Dunlap what the prisoner had said, and Mr. D. replied, "Very well, he may do as he pleases; if he does not like to be a witness we can do without him." *Perez* then cooled down, did not appear in such a passion as previously, and said that when he went before the judge he would tell the whole truth.

Mr. Dunlap said he should be happy to state any thing within his knowledge in relation to this matter; indeed he considered such a course to be his duty. After having had with *Perez* the conversation just alluded to by Mr. Badlam, and having noticed the state of his [Perez's] mind, he did not think it safe to leave the case for the government in its then state. He had therefore caused *Nicola Costa* to be brought in, and after telling him that he was under no obligation to state any thing, and that all he [the District Attorney] could promise him was that nothing he might say should be used against him, asked if he was willing to become a witness for the United States. The prisoner's reply was, "that they were all innocent, and that no robbery had ever been committed by them upon the Mexican." I then, said Mr. Dunlap, called in *Domingo Guzman*, and afterwards *Antonio Ferrer*, [the black cook] but found them both in the same story as *Costa*. As a last resort, I then sent for *Bernardo de Soto*, the mate, but succeeded as ill with him as with the others, I was influenced in sending for Costa and Guzman by considerations as to their youth; as regarded the black, by compassion for his ignorance and degraded condition; and I selected *de Soto* in consequence of his having performed the act of humanity which has been alluded to [saving the persons on board the Minerva.]

Mr. Child said the District Attorney had been influenced in this affair by the honorable feelings he supposed him to possess, and begged him to accept his (Mr. C.'s) sincere thanks for the course pursued.

Mr. Dunlap in reply to Mr. Child, said that when the offer of becoming a witness was made to de Soto, the latter returned for answer that he was willing to testify, but could only do so to his own innocence. He (Mr. D.) thought de Soto answered evasively, and therefore immediately ceased conversing with him.

Mr. Hillard arose and addresed the Jury for two hours in the most eloquent manner.

You are called upon to exercise your vocation in a case, a parallel to which we should seek in vain, in the criminal annals of this, and I had almost said in those of any other state or country. It is a serious thing gentlemen, to sit in judgment, for life or death upon a single person. Such a duty requires the most clear state of the understanding, the most careful attention to facts, lest through rashness or prejudice we pass sentence on the innocent, and commit judicial murder. Instead of one, you are now called upon to decide the fate of *twelve* persons. By your verdict, will it be determined whether the individuals who now sit before you in the fullness of life shall continue to exist or taste the bitterness of Death. The extraordinary spectacle is now presented of a number of prisoners tallying exactly with the jury.

Mr. Hillard after arguing upon the improbability of the prisoners being the crew that robbed the Mexican, and giving an interesting account of Bernardo de Soto's act of humanity in relieving the American ship on fire, concluded with an eloquent appeal in behalf of Antonio Ferrer, the black, and the boy Costa.

If, gentlemen, said he, you deem with me that the crew of the *Panda* (supposing her to have robbed the Mexican) were merely servants of the captain, you cannot convict them. But if you do not agree with me, then all that remains for me to do is to address a few words to you in the way of mercy.—It does not seem to me that the good of society requires the death of all these men, the sacrifice of such a hecatomb of human victims, or that the sword of the law should fall till it is clogged with massacre. *Antonio Ferrer* is plainly but a servant. He is set down as a free black in the ship's papers, but that is no proof that he is free. Were he a slave he would in all probability be represented as free, and this for obvious reasons. He is in all probability a slave, and a native African, as the tattooing on his face proves beyond a doubt. At any rate he is but a servant. Now will you make misfortune pay the penalty of guilt? Do not, I entreat you, lightly condemn this man to death. Do not throw him in to make up the dozen. The regard for human life is one of the most prominent proofs of a civilized state of society. The Sultan of Turkey may place women in sacks and throw them into the *Bosphorus* without exciting more than an hour's additional conversation at Constantinople. But in our country it is different. You well remember the excitement produced by the abduction and death of a single individual; the convulsion which ensued, the effect of which will long be felt in our political institutions. You will ever find that the more a nation becomes civilized, the greater becomes the regard for human life. There is in the eye, the form, and heaven directed countenance of man something holy that forbids he should be rudely touched.

The instinct of life is great. The light of the sun even in chains, is pleasant; and life, though supported but by the damp exhalations of a dungeon, is desirable. Often too we cling with added tenacity to life in proportion as we are deprived of all that makes existence to be coveted.

> The weariest and most loathed worldly life
> That age, ache, penury and imprisonment
> Can lay on Nature, is a Paradise
> To that we fear of *Death.*

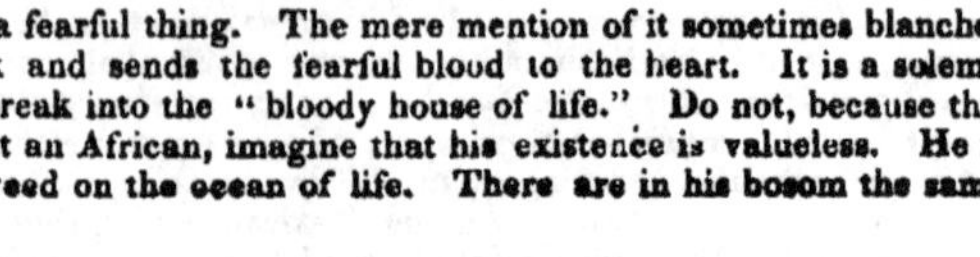

Antonio on the Top-Gallant Yard.

Death is a fearful thing. The mere mention of it sometimes blanches the cheek and sends the fearful blood to the heart. It is a solemn thing to break into the "bloody house of life." Do not, because this man is but an African, imagine that his existence is valueless. He is no drift weed on the ocean of life. There are in his bosom the same social sympathies that animate our own. He has nerves to feel pain, and a heart to throb with human affections, even as you have. His life, to establish the law, or to further the ends of justice, is not required. *Taken*, it is to us of no value; given to him it is above the price of rubies.

And *Costa*, the cabin boy, only 15 years of age when this crime was committed. Shall he die? Shall the sword fall upon his neck? Some of you are advanced in years. You may have children. Suppose the news had reached you that your son was under trial for his life in a foreign country—(and every cabin boy who leaves this port

The Carpenter applying the Match to a Bag of Powder in the Magazine.

may be placed in the situation of this prisoner)—suppose you were told that he had been *executed* because his captain and officers had violated the laws of a distant land;—what would be your feelings? I cannot tell, but I believe the feelings of all of you would be the same, and that you would exclaim with the Hebrew, "My son! my son! would to God that I had died for thee." This boy *has* a father; let the form of that father rise up before you and plead in your hearts for his offspring. Perhaps he has a mother, and a home. Think of the lengthened shadow that must have been cast over that home by his absence. Think of his mother, during those hours of wretchedness

when she has felt hope darkening into disappointment, next into anxiety, and from anxiety to despair. How often may she have stretched forth her hands in supplication, and asked, even the winds of heaven, to bring her tidings of him who was away? Let the supplications of that mother touch your hearts and shield their object from the law.

Mr. Child closed the Defence on the part of the Prisoners in an ingenious and elaborate argument of twelve hours.

He commenced by reading numerous statements showing how extremely difficult it was to identify persons, and what little dependence could be placed on evidence of this sort. He cited many authorities for the defence. He argued at great length upon the statements of the government witness Perez, and animadverted strongly against the manner in which he had given his testimony, and the great degree of hatred and revenge he exhibited on the stand; his utter want of veracity in saying he could not read his alphabet, but, after being pressed on that point, read whole sentences fluently; his saying rum had been given him at Fernando Po, and telling since "what he had said was all a lie." He spoke strongly in favor of the crew because there was no rule of division; the Captain and Mate keeping as much of the plunder as they chose. And Captain Trotter had not treated the crew of the Panda as Pirates, having kept them in irons but a short time. The statement of Bernardo De Soto's sitting up all night to make a false log-book should have no weight; if he had, it would be produced here. In the printed statement of Captain Butman, the Panda's figure head is said to be very large, with a horn of plenty on it; the witness Silvera, who saw it in the river Nazareth, says there was nothing carved on it. Mr. Quentin says it was off smooth like the stern of a boat. With respect to the capture of the Schooner, something explanatory of the conduct of her company may be said. Being unexpectedly and suddenly surrounded with a squadron of hostile boats, they fled for safety;—and, if they did attempt to blow her up, there is nothing very blameable. Many a brave spirit, incapable of yielding to defeat, has ascended from the ruins of his gallant vessel.

After arguing and endeavouring to refute and lessen the weight of the government testimony, he concluded by making a powerful appeal in favor of Antonio Ferrer and the boy Costa.

Mr. Dunlap, District Attorney, closed the cause on the part of the government in a most eloquent argument of six hours.

He began by saying that there was no doubt the Mexican was robbed by pirates. The great question was whether the captain and crew of the Panda were the individuals who committed the robbery. She sailed from Havana about the 20th. The witnesses prove that Captain Gibert and Bernardo de Soto were her chief officers, and the prisoners at the bar were all of her crew. The crew of the Mexican make this probability certain by identifying some of the prisoners who were proved to be of the Panda's crew. This is not circumstantial evidence, it is proof positive.—Mr. D. argued that the Panda sailed with the intention of committing piracies; Bernardo De Soto was not the real owner; he stands in their shoes; the real owners are veiled. The instructions are not signed; there is piracy in every line of them. The contract with the Captain is in the same hand writing as the unsigned instructions. The cargo of the vessel is worth only $10,000, and going to Africa to buy 450 slaves. The cargo would not pay the wages of the crew for 10 months. She was to get the $30,000 to buy the slaves by robbing vessels, without doubt. With these instructions Captain Gibert is told to sail from St. Thomas in ballast, to enter with great secresy into the harbor of Matanzas by night, and hold intercourse with certain persons indicated in his instructions. He was allowed to cruise where he pleased. He was left without any control but his own will. The slave trade is the twin-brother of piracy, for all the piracies of our day are committed by slave dealers. By the large share of the money kept by the Captain it proves that it was reserved for the owners. At the time the figure head was altered, no news had reached Africa of the piracy. He had it altered to elude pursuit when the news did come. It shows the prisoners were conscious of guilt by throwing the money overboard.

After drawing the attention of the jury to the boy Costa and Antonio Ferrer, he concluded by passing an eloquent eulogium on the conduct of Captain Trotter and the British navy generally.

Judge Story, in a luminous *Charge* of six hours summed up the evidence on both sides of the cause.. The papers, charts and documents were given to the jury and they retired to agree upon a verdict.

A SECTION OF BLUNT'S CHART OF THE COAST OF AFRICA, SHOWING THE HAUNTS OF THE PIRATES.

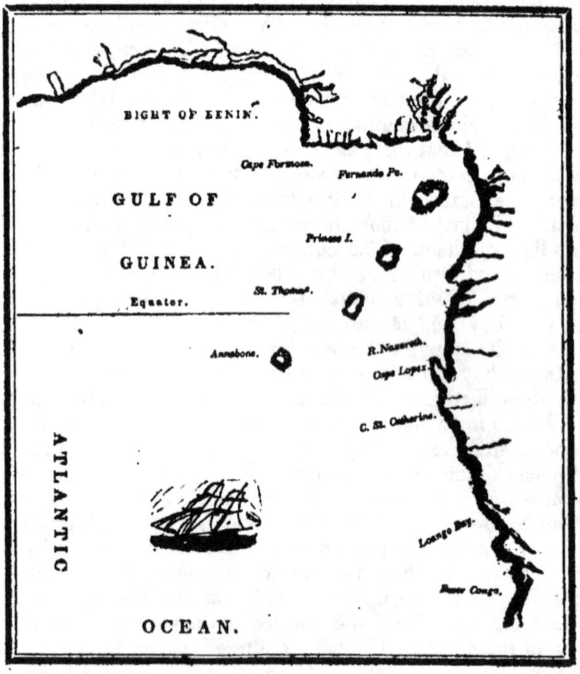

CPSIA information can be obtained
at www.ICGtesting.com
Printed in the USA
BVHW011721050619
550105BV00053B/510/P

9 780353 644465